Dear Parents, Carers, and Teachers,

This book, "I Feel Great", has one word per page in alphabetical order. They can be used for, but certainly not limited to discuss:

English – letters and words recognition. Also how font types make same letters appear different.

Geometry – shapes and pattern recognition.

Psychology – humans experience a range of emotions, and everyone has permission to feel all of it. Both boys and girls are allowed to express themselves.

Art – colour choices and combinations.

And of course:

Down time – just sit and enjoy the process of colouring!!

Amazing
Beautiful
Caring
Daring
Excited
Fierce
Great
Happy
Independent
Joyful
Kind
Loving
Magical
Nifty
Open
Proud
Quietness
Rested
Super
Terrific
Understood
Validated
Wonderful
Excellent
Yippee
Zestful

I feel...

AMAZING

I feel...

BEAUTIFUL

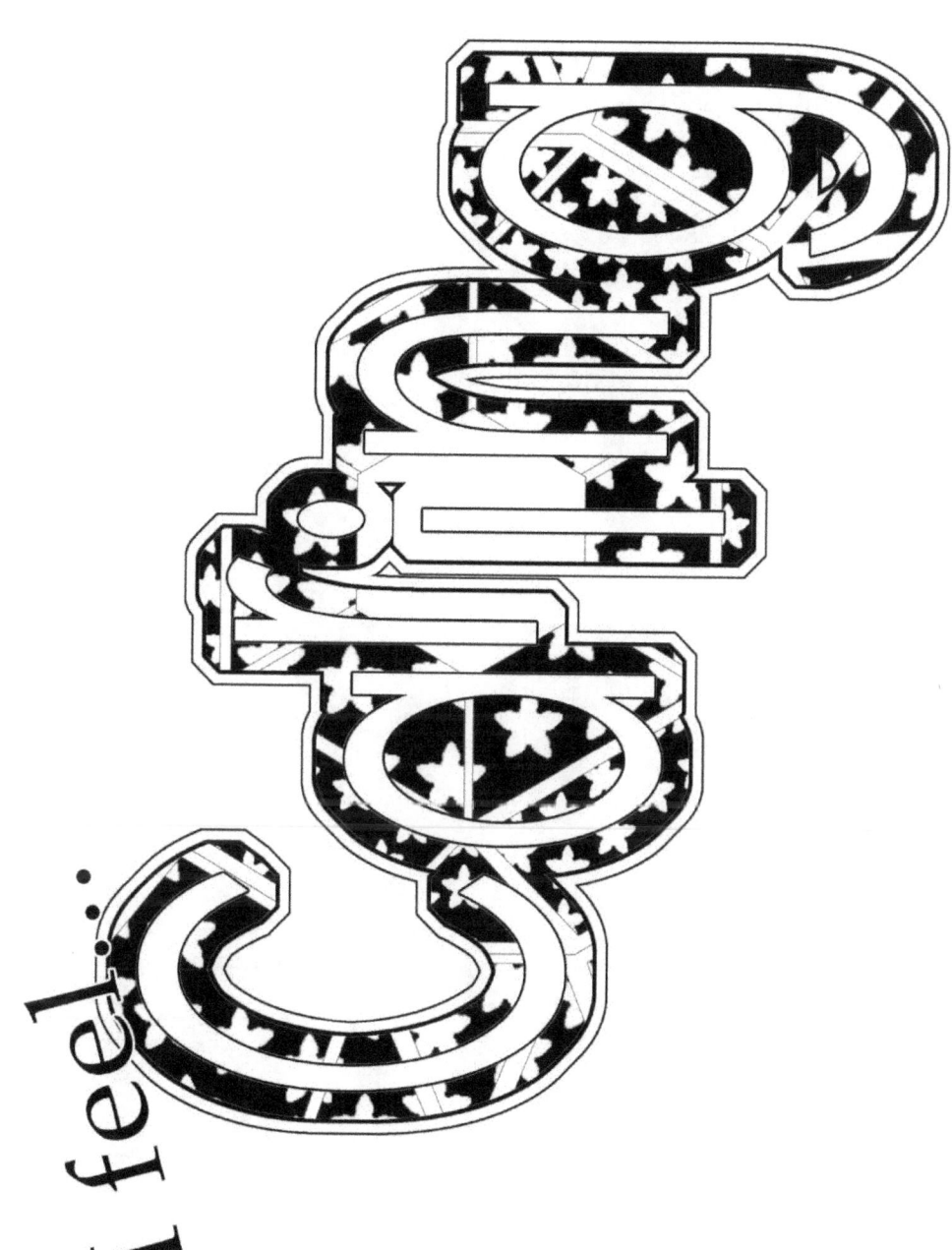

I feel...

I feel...

I feel...

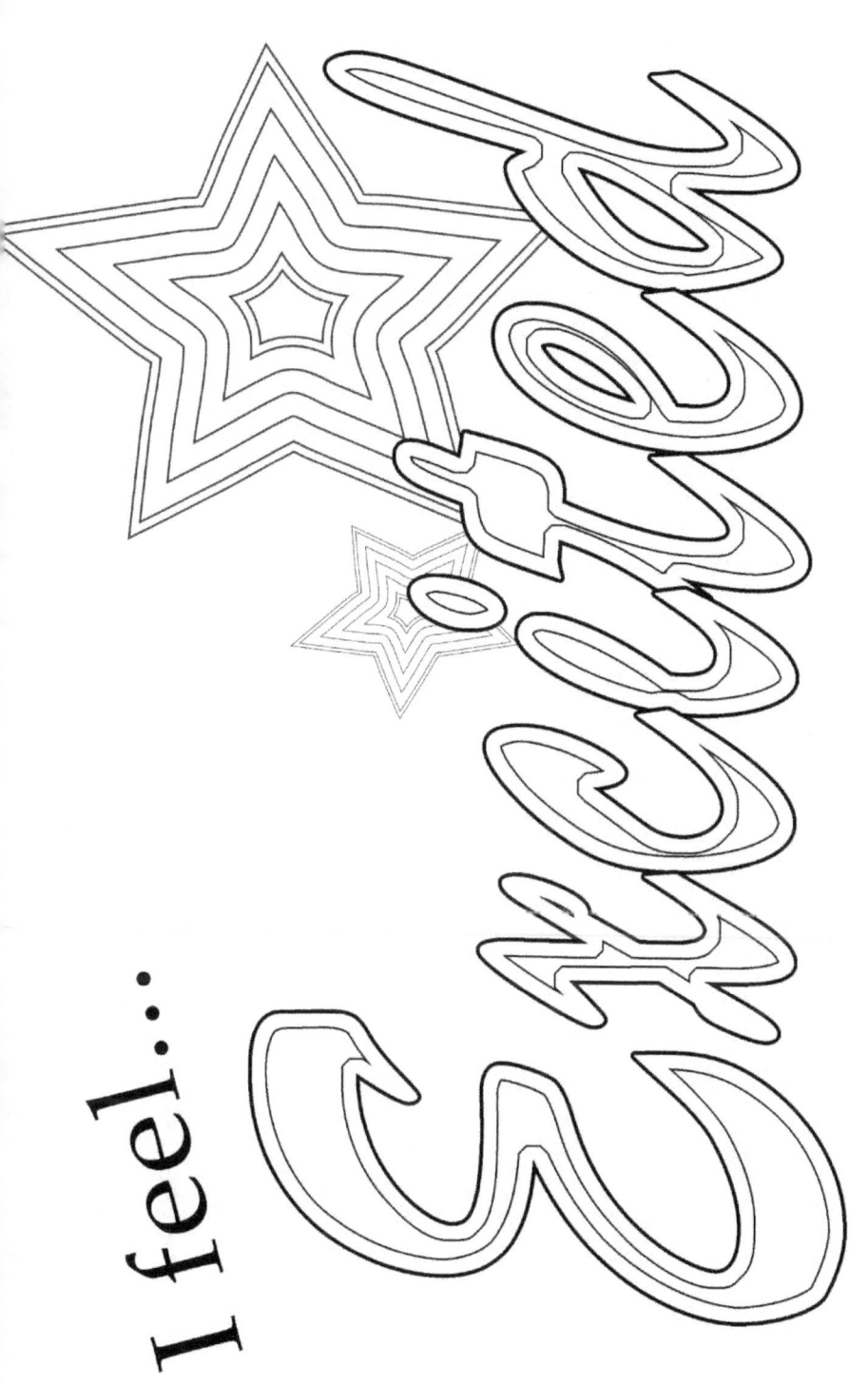

I feel...

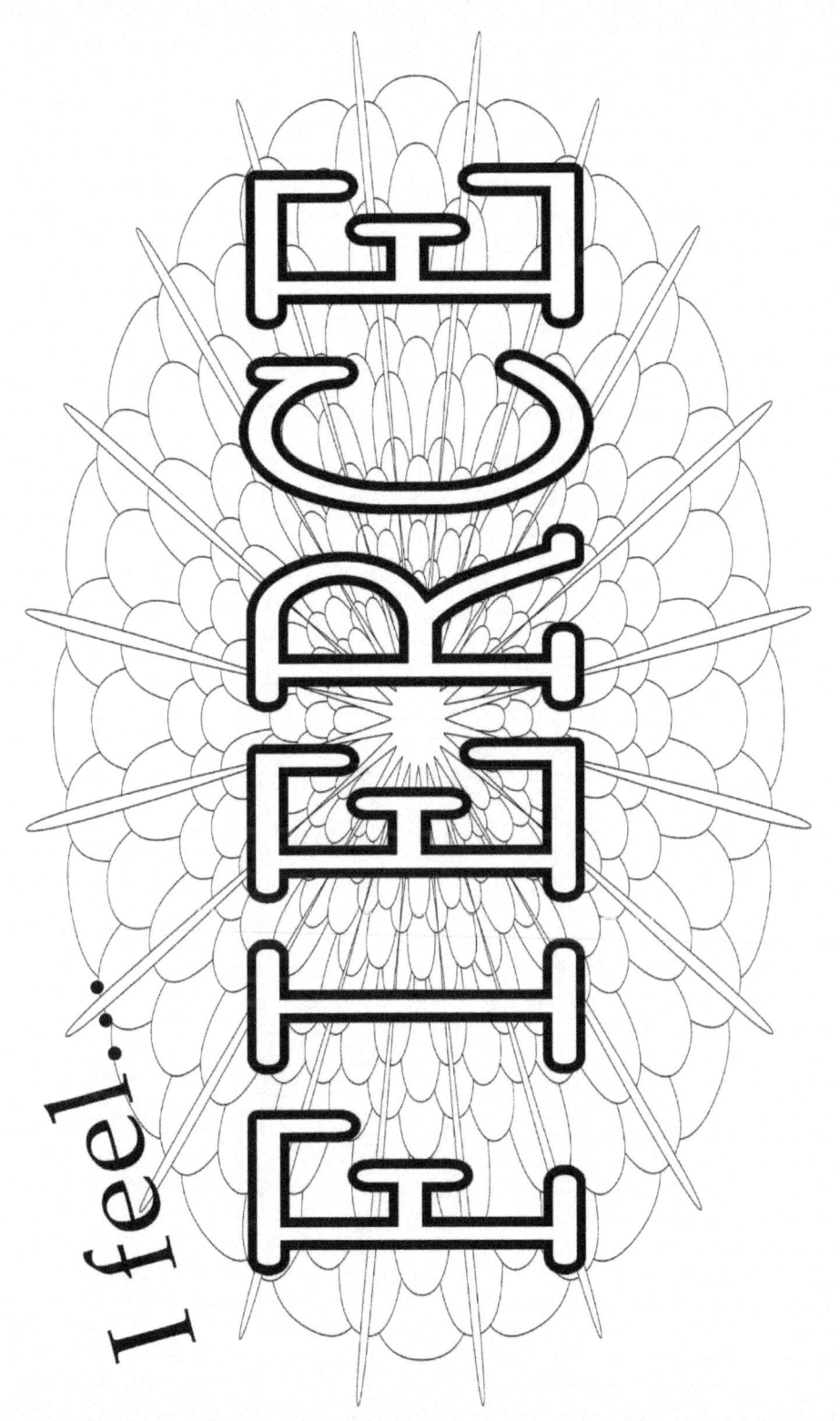

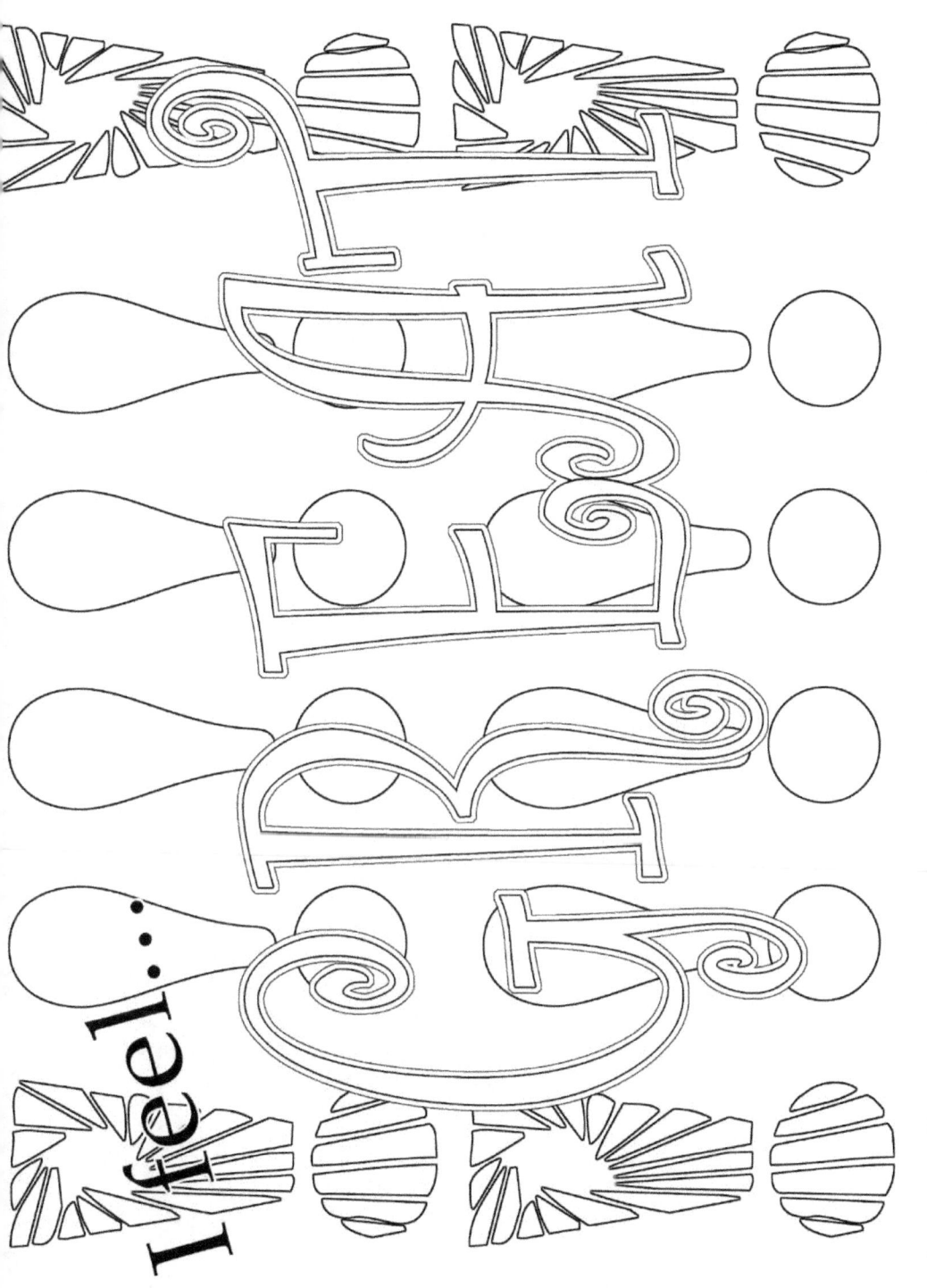

I feel...

I feel...

I feel...

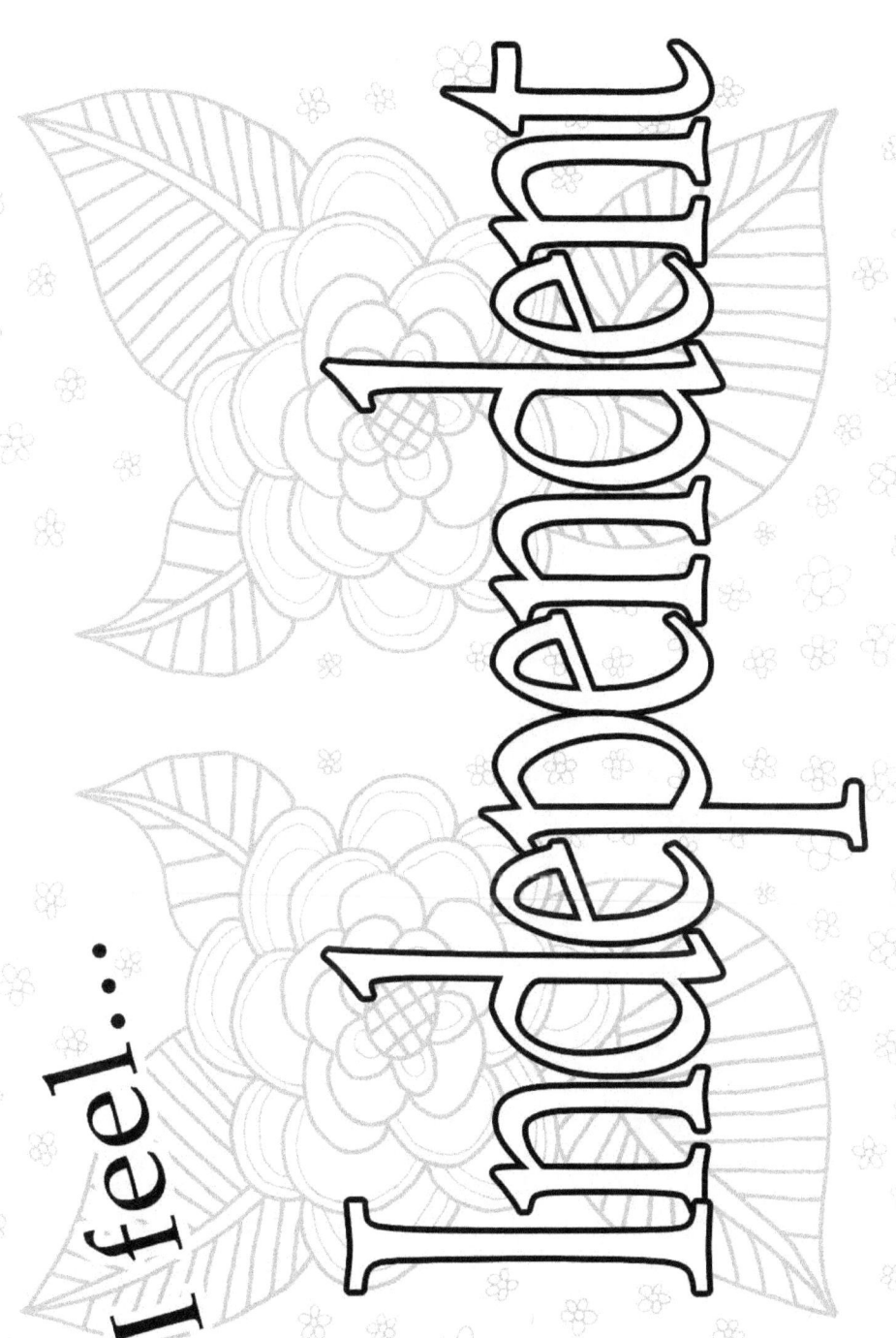

Independent

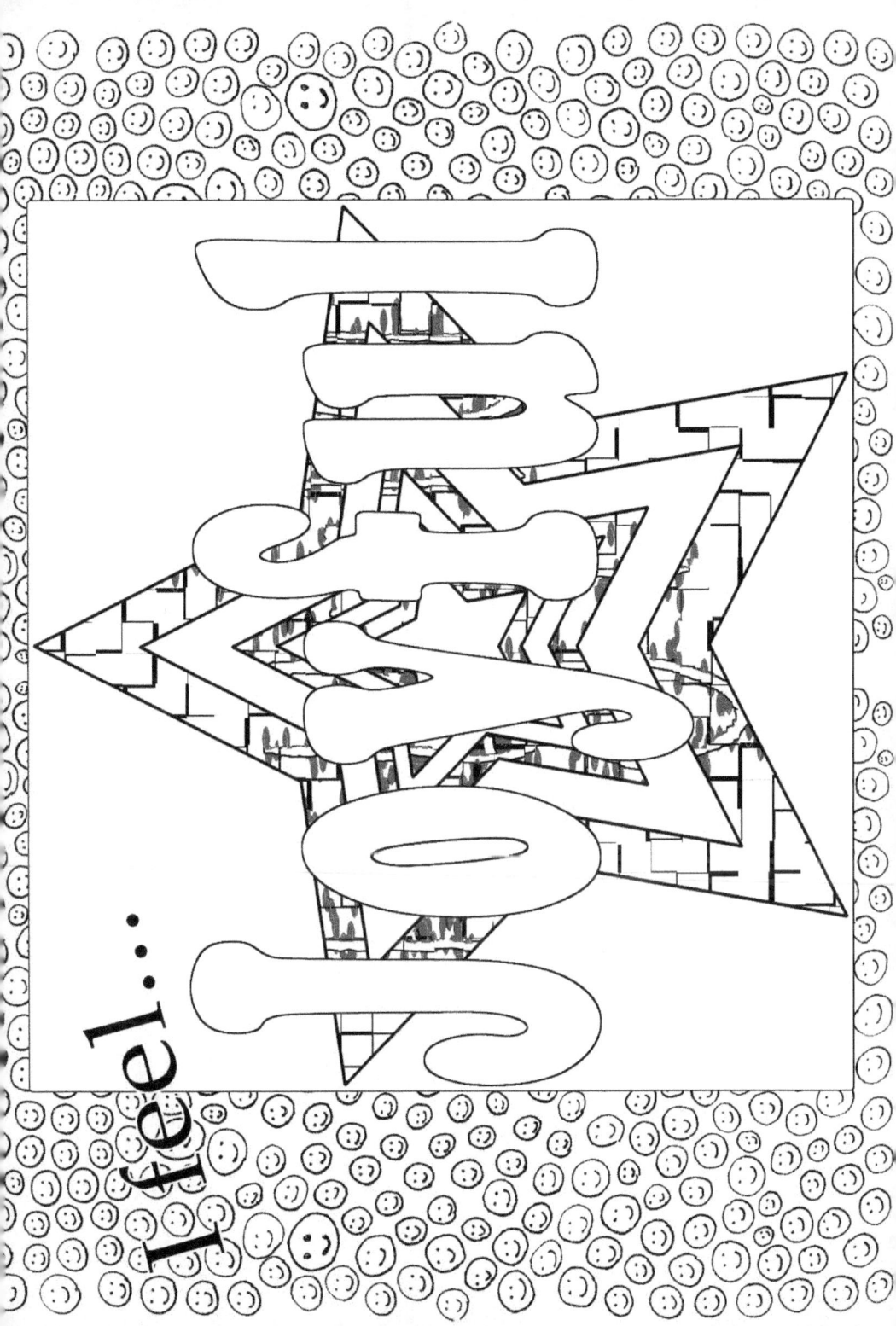

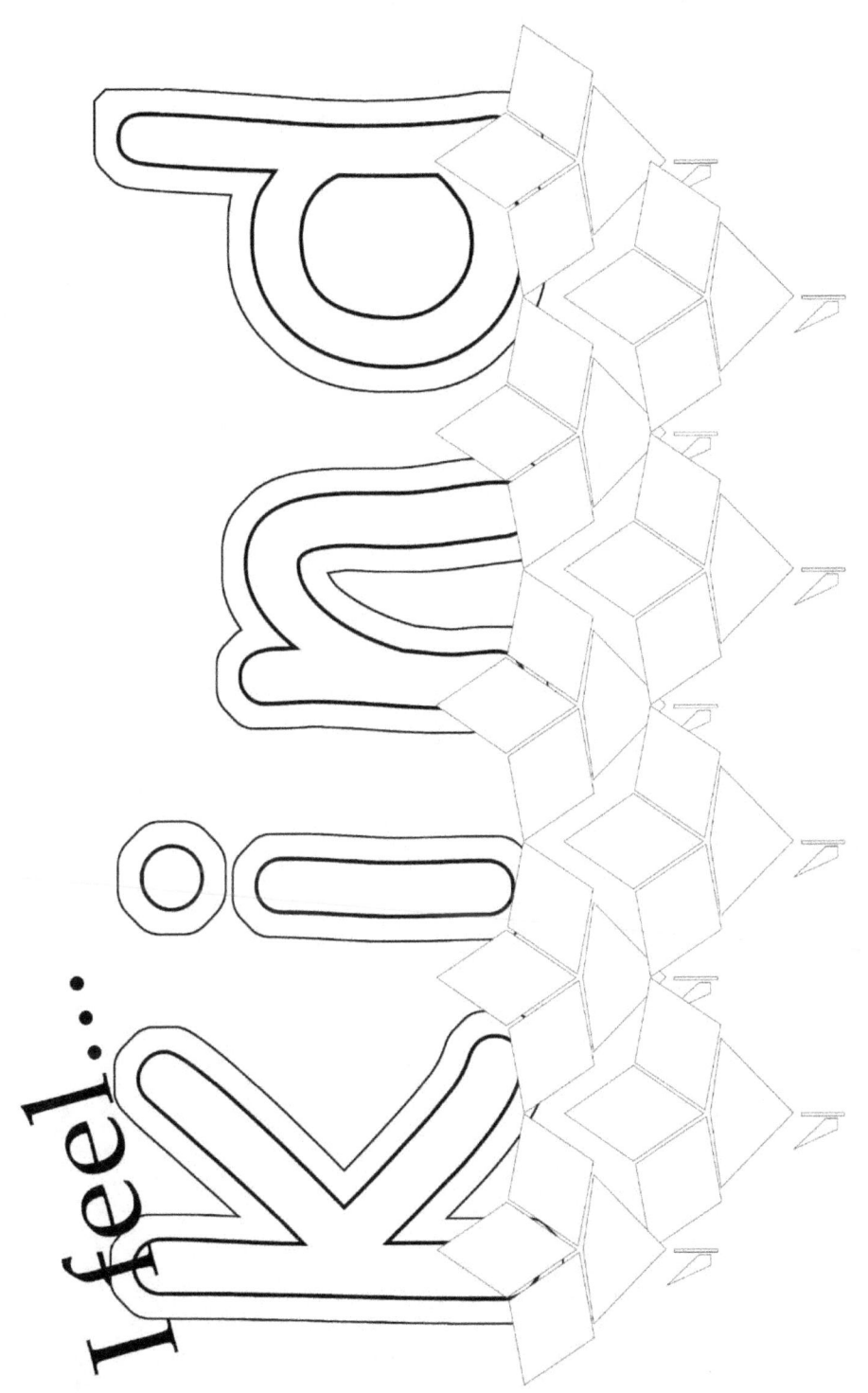

I feel...

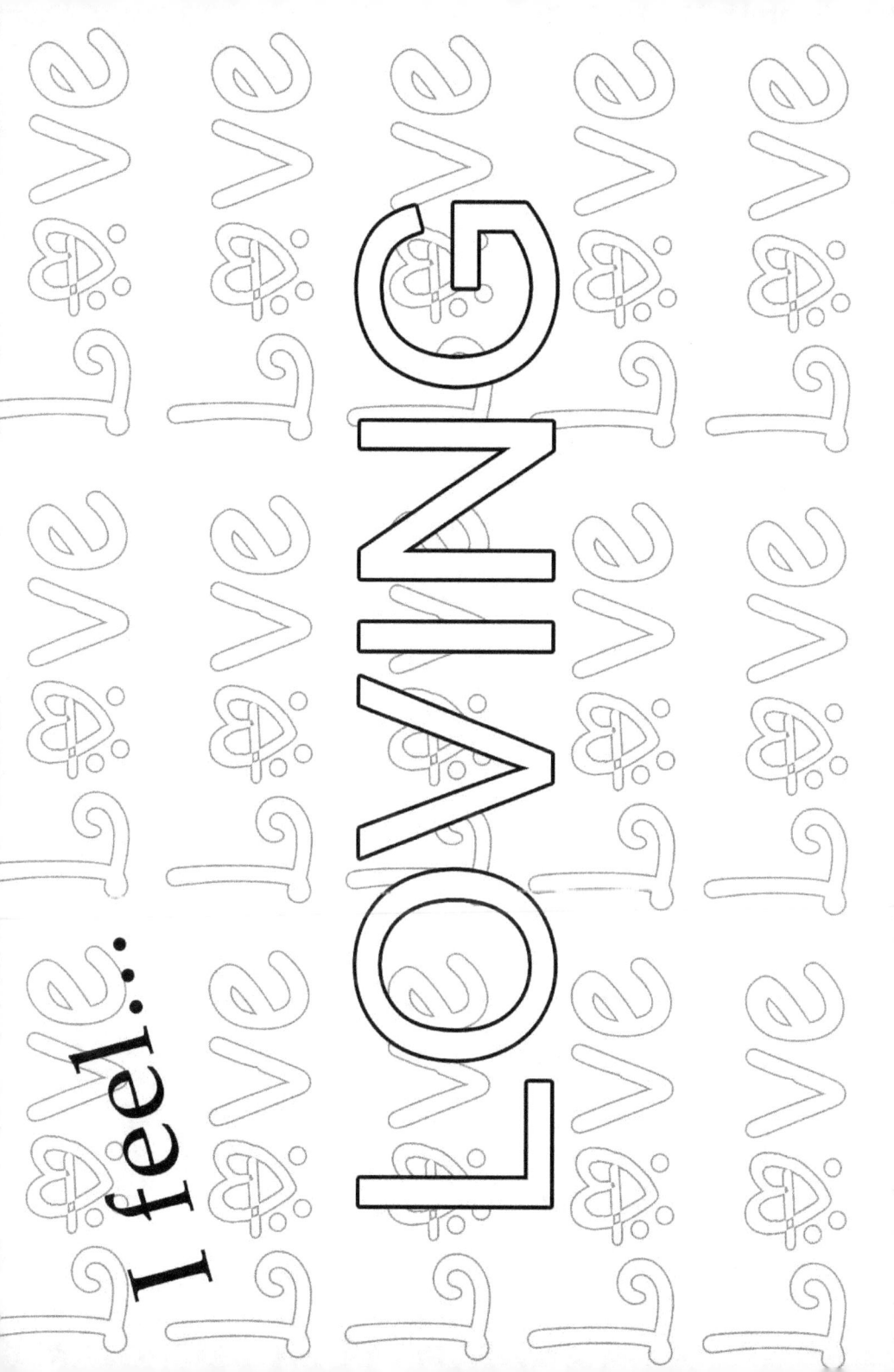

I feel...

LOVING

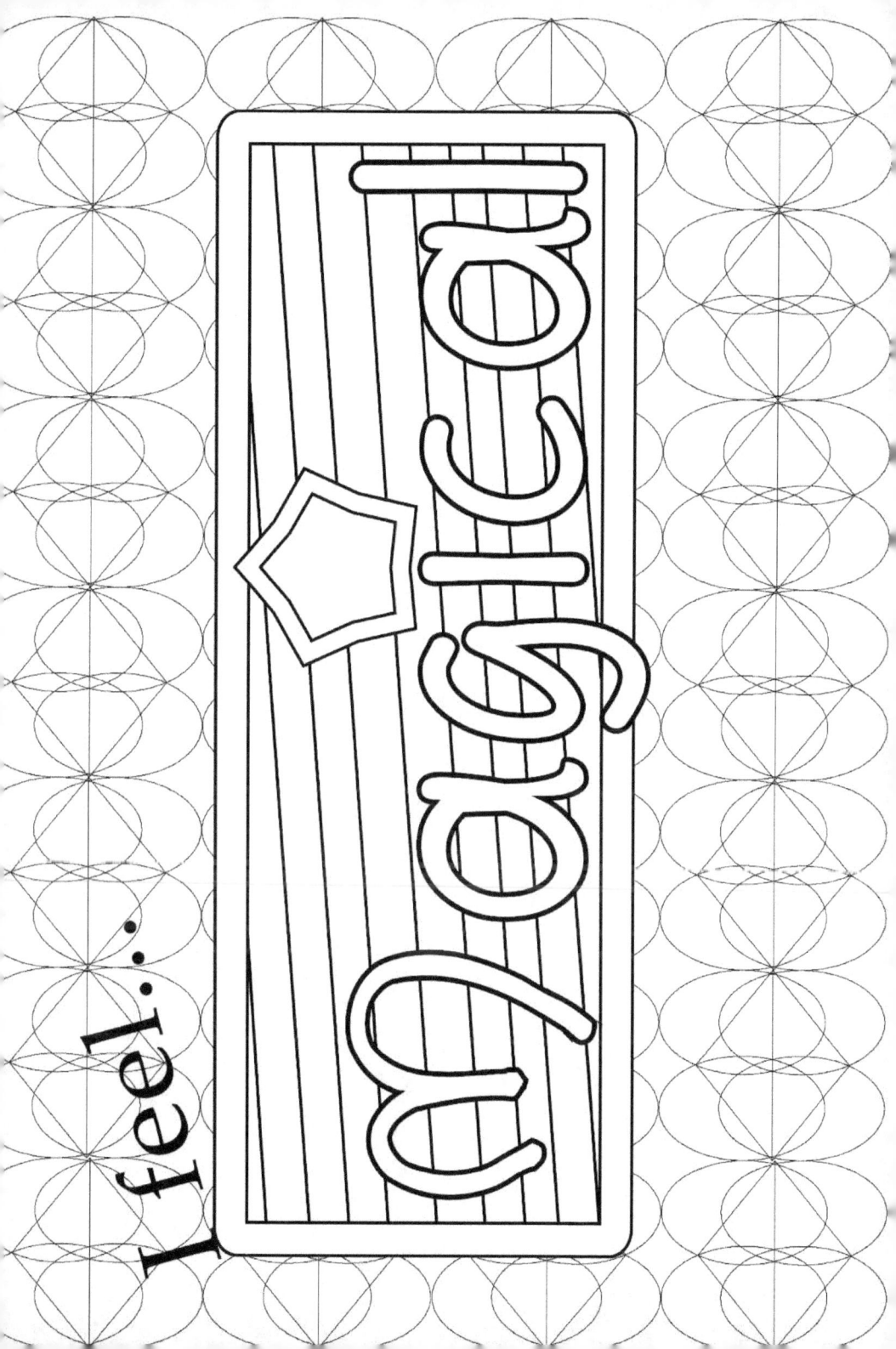

I feel...

Magical

I feel...

I feel...

HAPPY

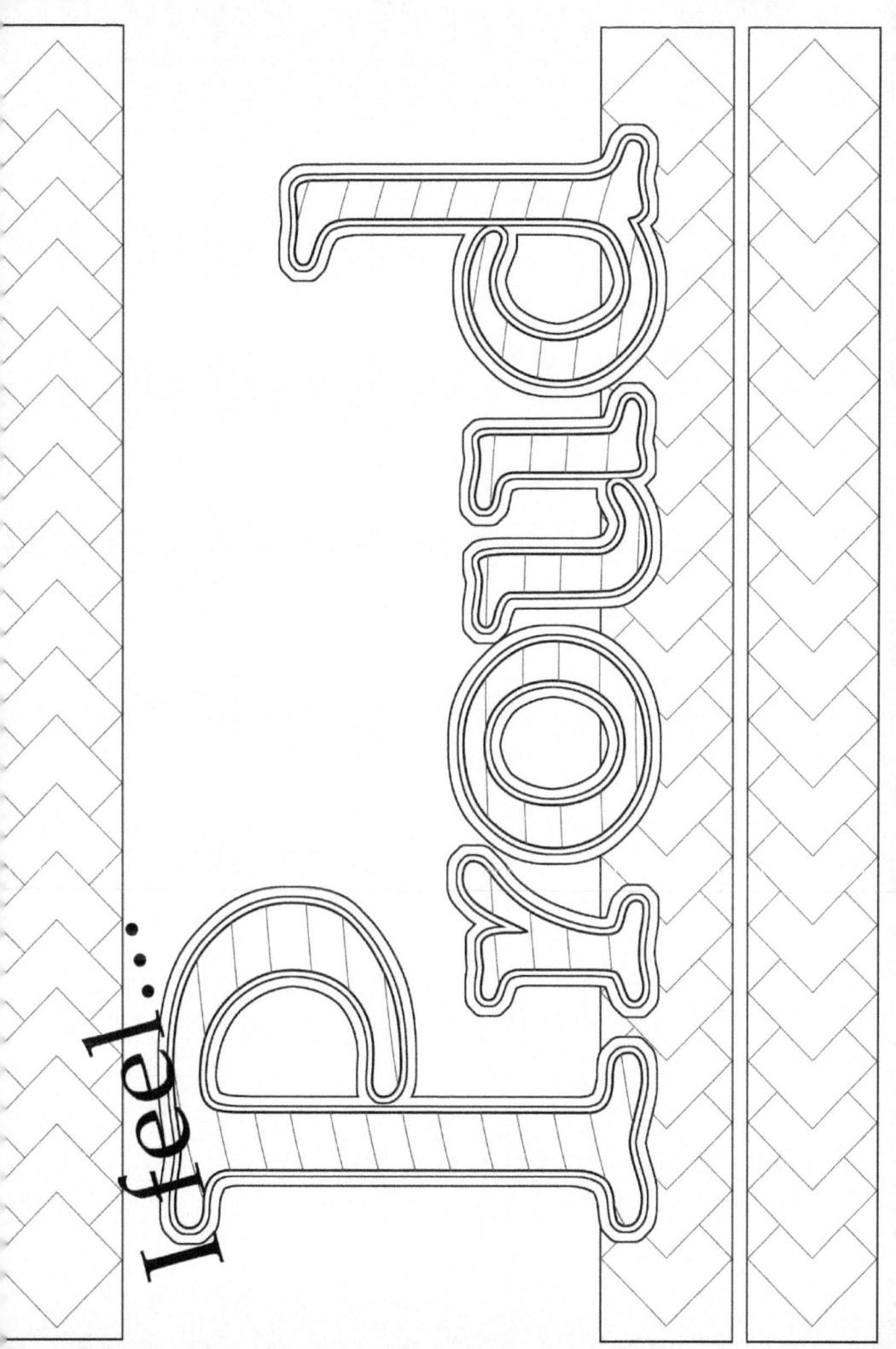

I feel... Proud

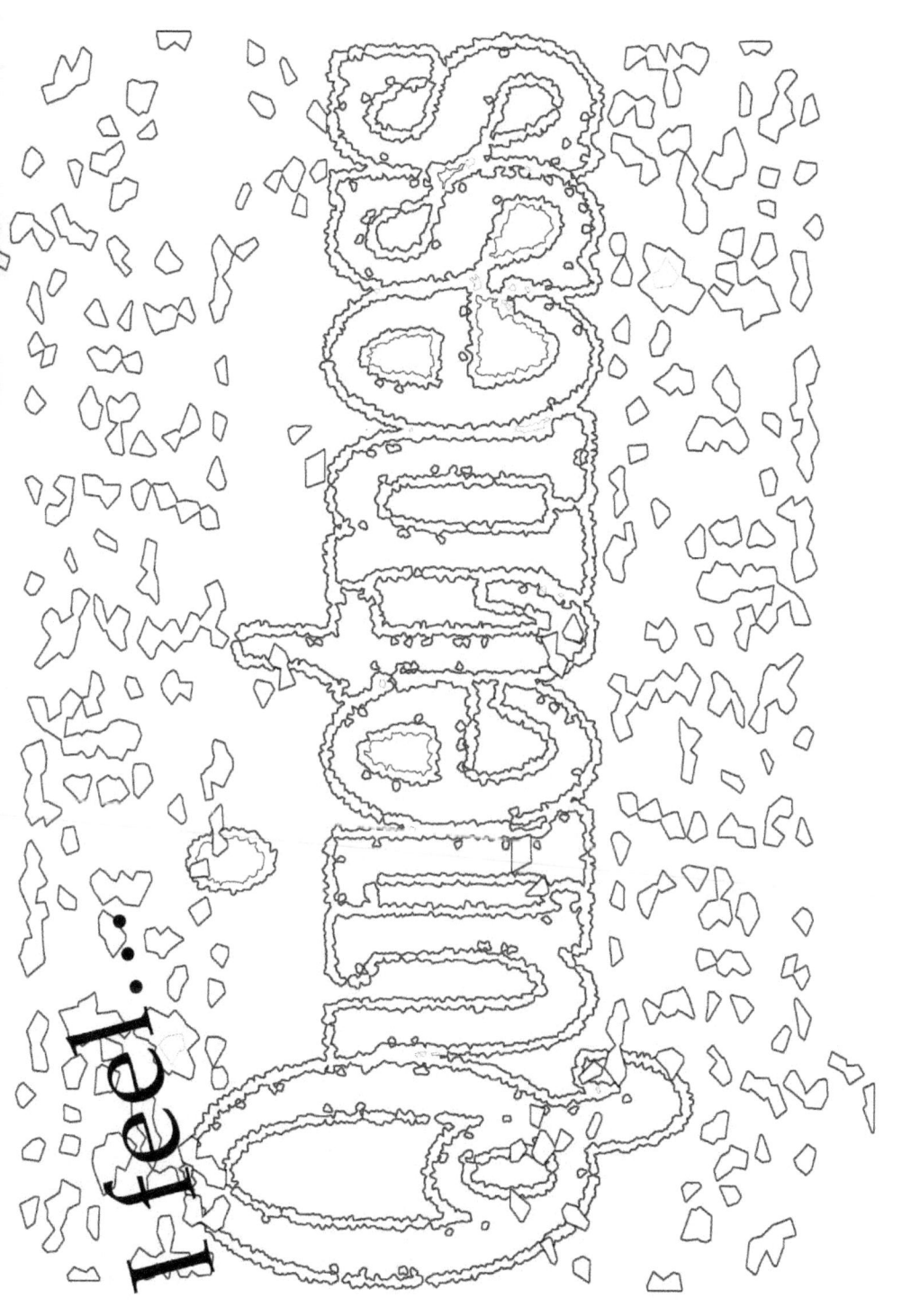

I feel...

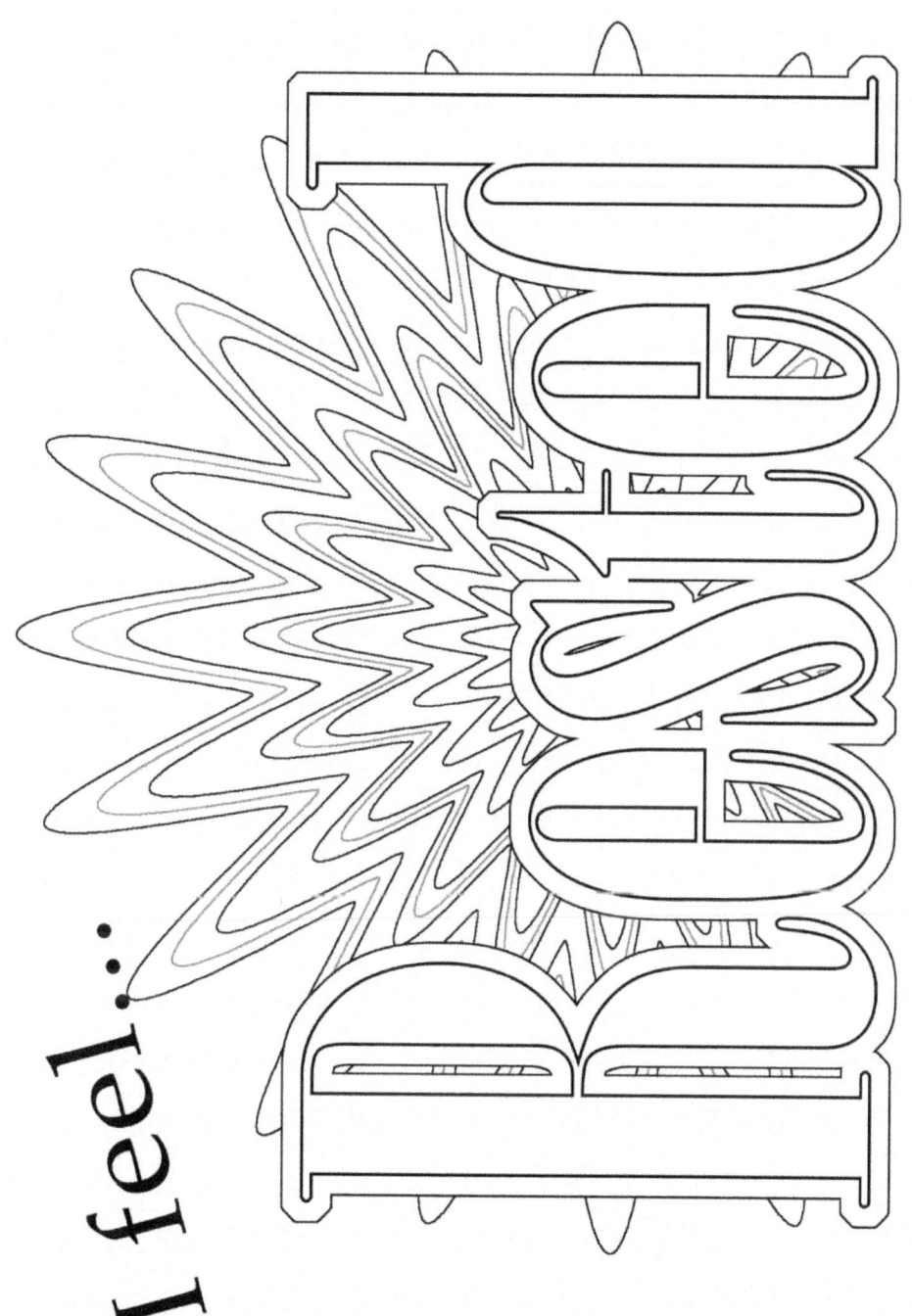

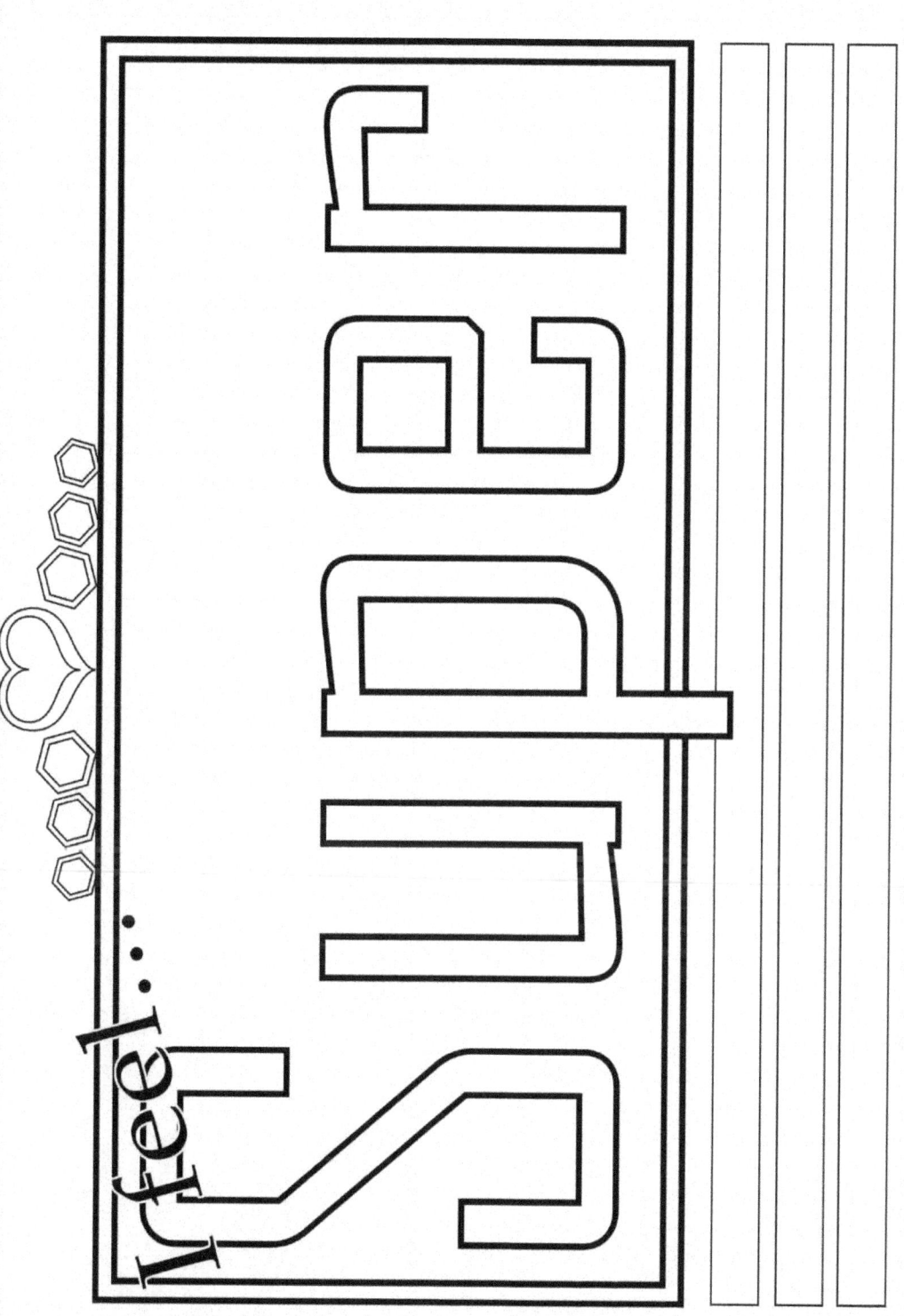

I feel......super

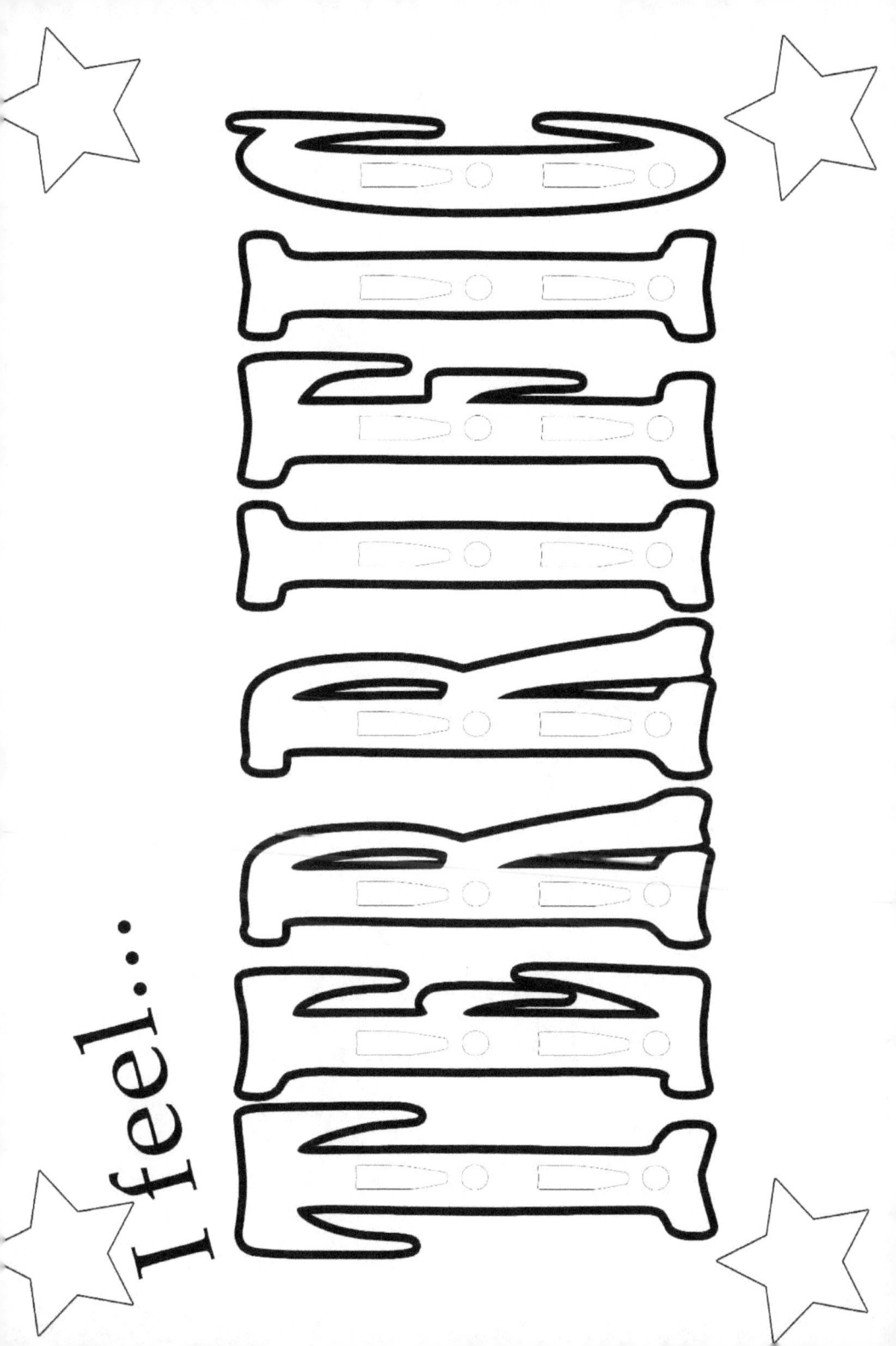

I feel... TERRIFIED

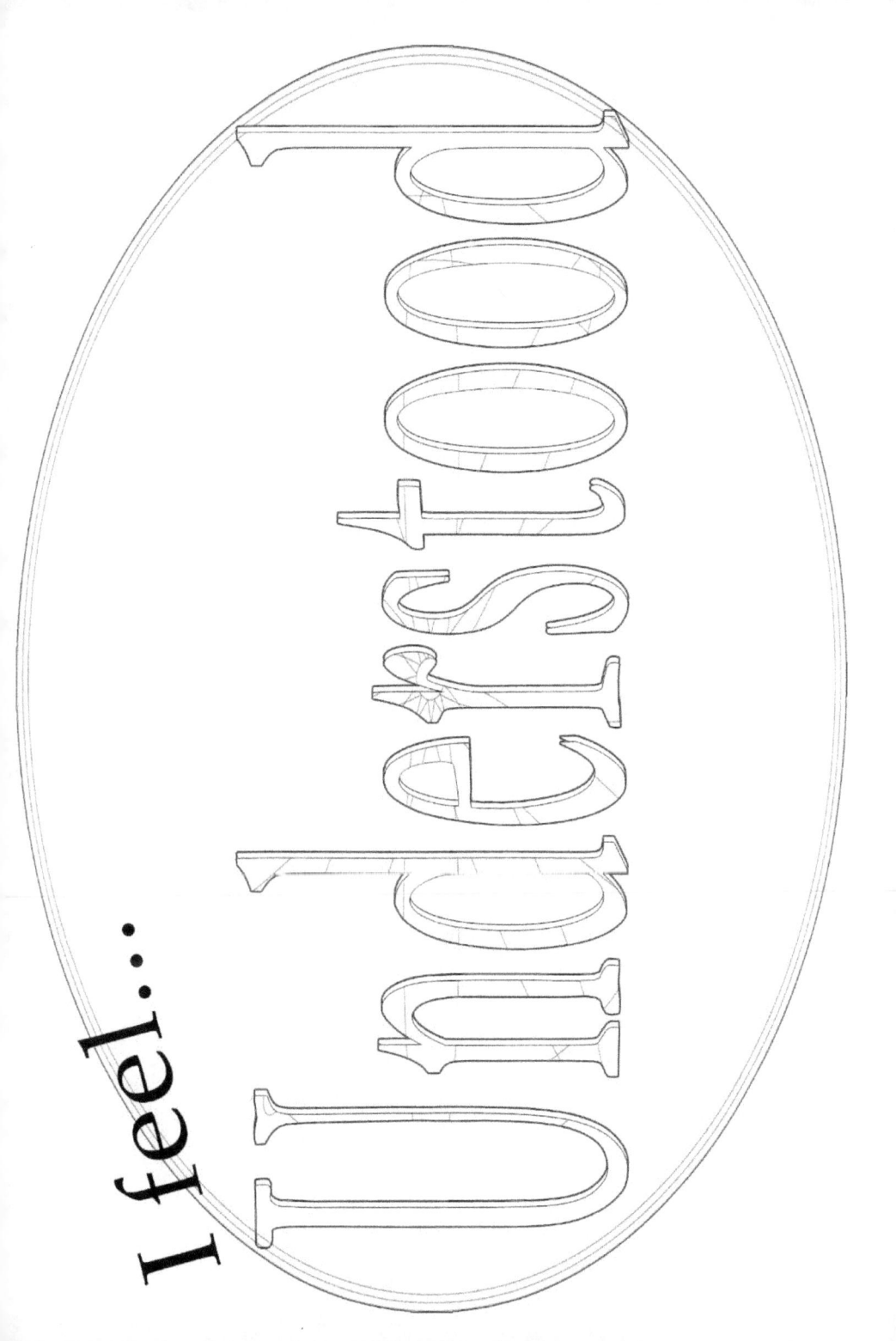

I feel... Understood

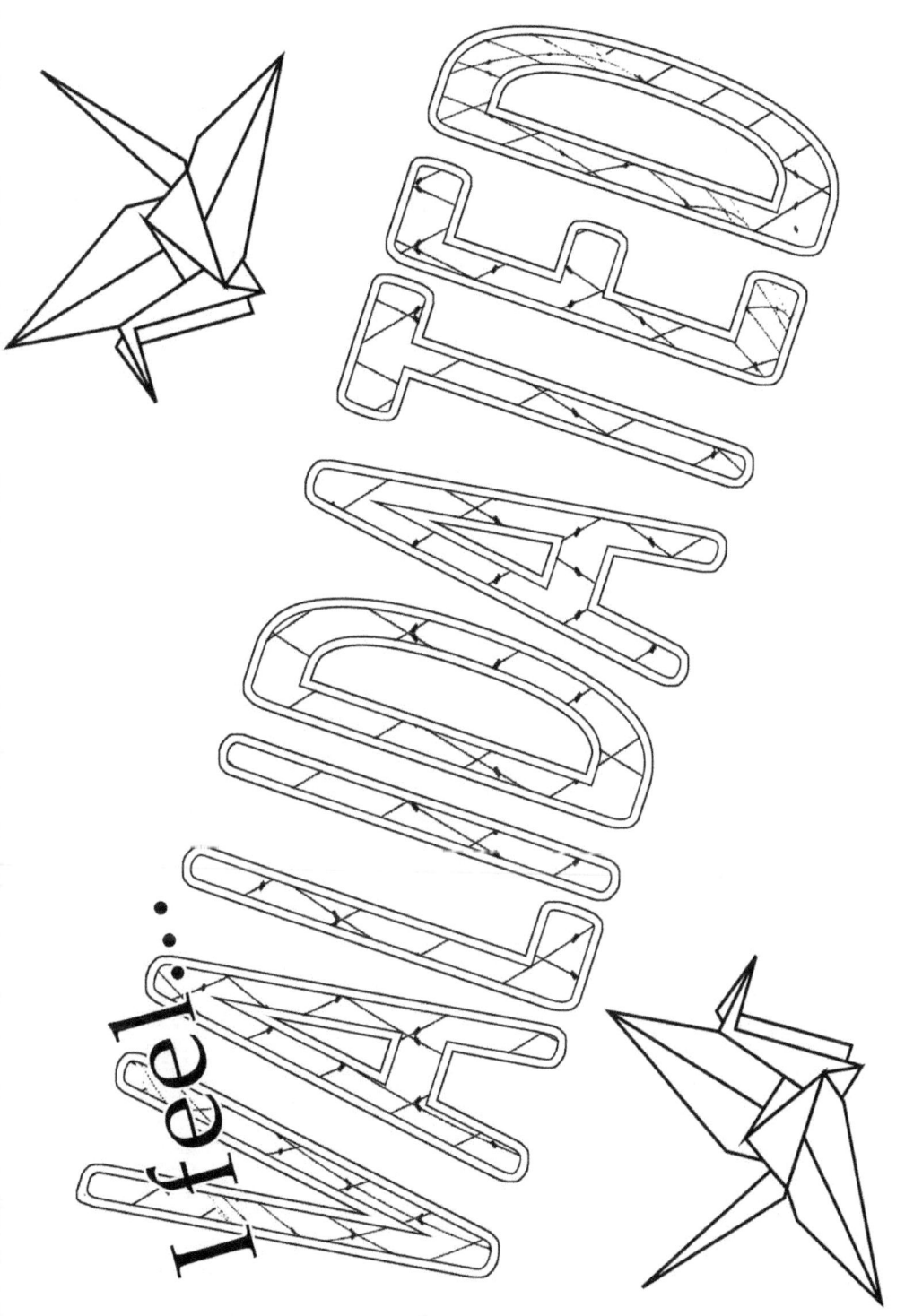

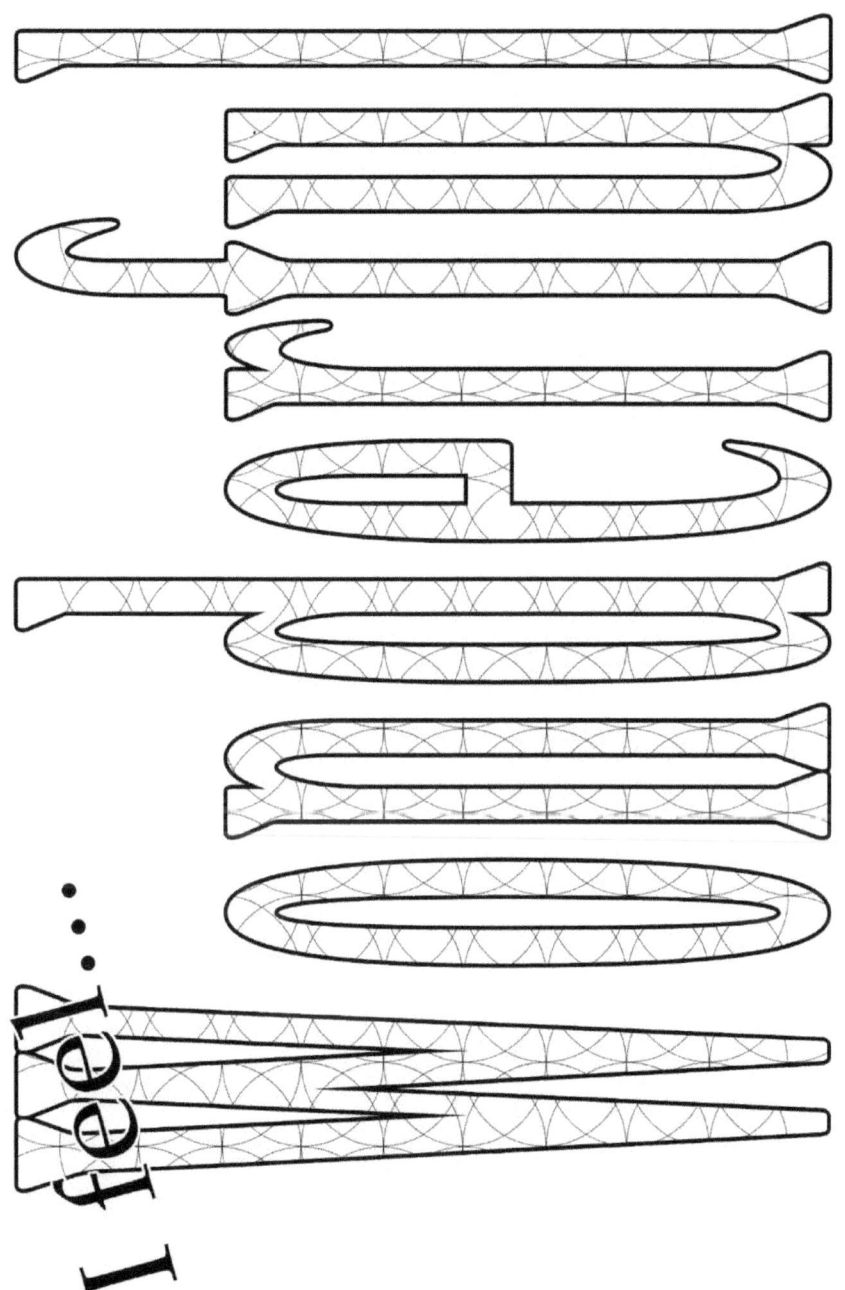

I feel...

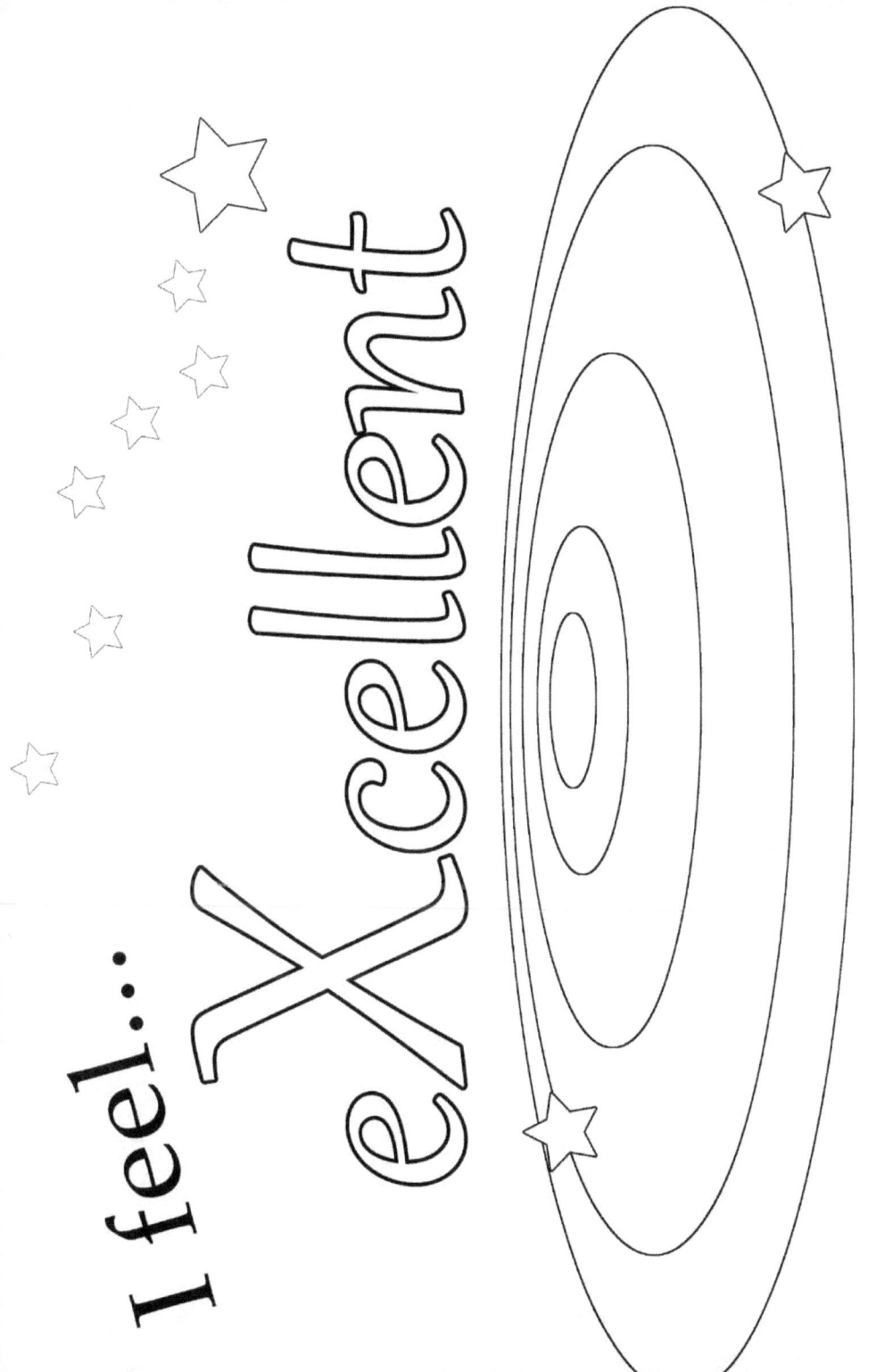
I feel... eXcellent

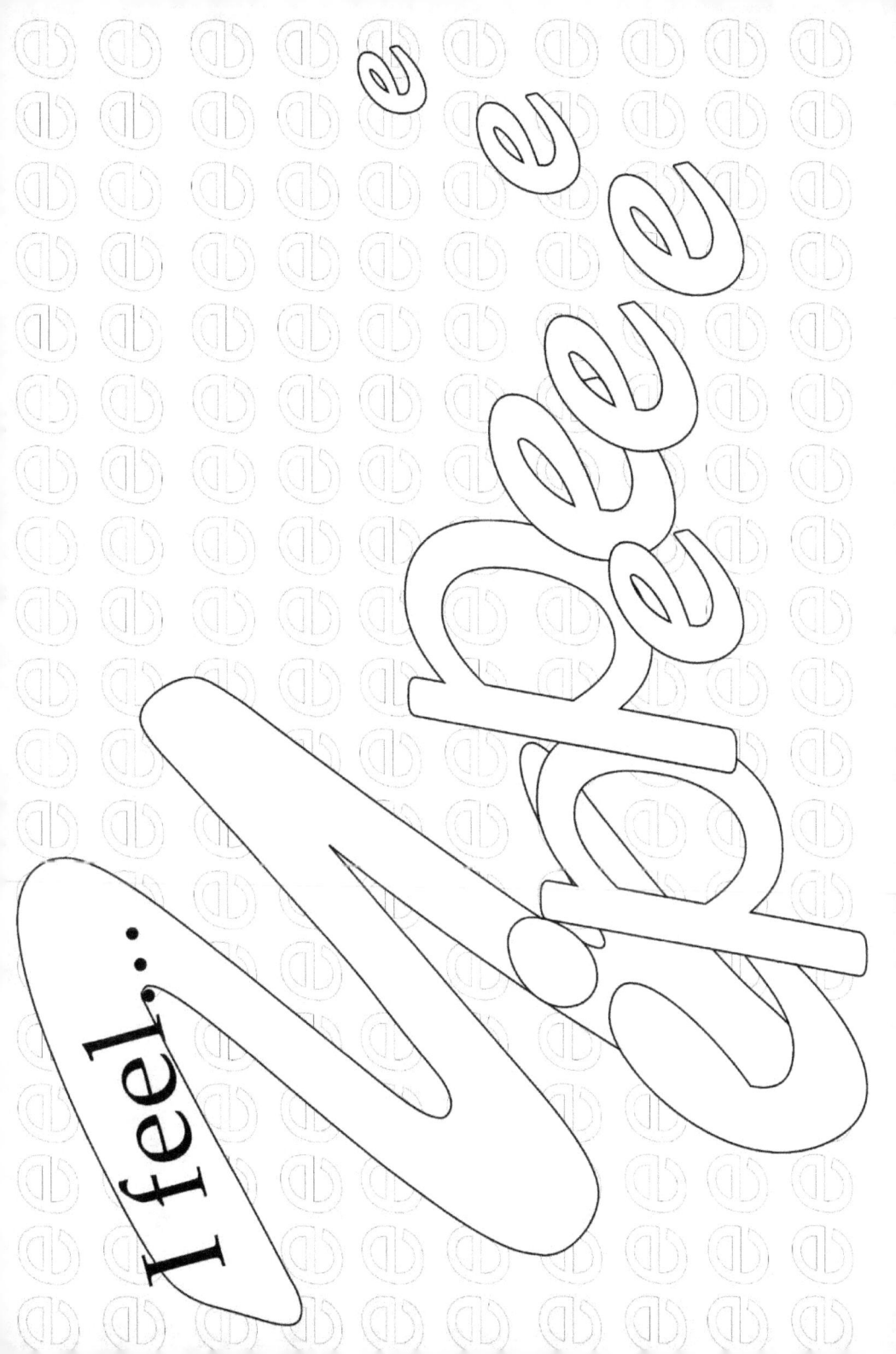

I feel... carefree

I feel...

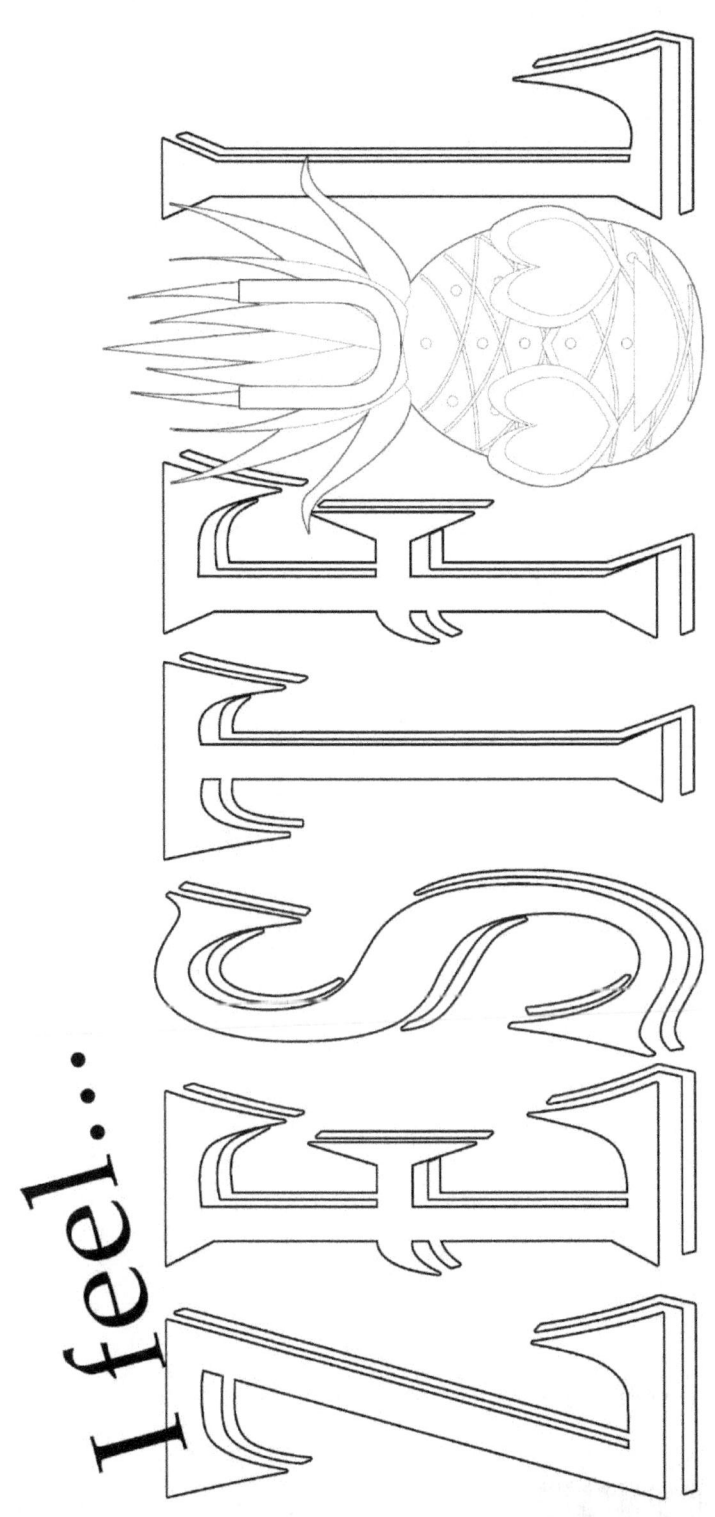

FRUSTRATED